SMART ABOUT...

PIERRE~AUGUSTE RENOIR

PAINTINGS THAT SMILE

by
Winter Lind

I'm like a piece of cork thrown in the water and carried by the current. I let my painting take me where it will!

written and illustrated by
TRUE KELLEY

Grosset & Dunlap • New York

With thanks to Klare Nevins and Dorothy Parsons—T.K.

GROSSET & DUNLAP
Published by the Penguin Group
Penguin Group (USA) Inc., 375 Hudson Street, New York, New York 10014, U.S.A.
Penguin Group (Canada), 10 Alcorn Avenue, Toronto, Ontario, Canada M4V 3B2
(a division of Pearson Penguin Canada Inc.)
Penguin Books Ltd, 80 Strand, London WC2R 0RL, England
Penguin Ireland, 25 St Stephen's Green, Dublin 2, Ireland
(a division of Penguin Books Ltd)
Penguin Group (Australia), 250 Camberwell Road, Camberwell, Victoria 3124, Australia
(a division of Pearson Australia Group Pty Ltd)
Penguin Books India Pvt Ltd, 11 Community Centre, Panchsheel Park, New Delhi - 110 017, India
Penguin Group (NZ), Cnr Airborne and Rosedale Roads, Albany, Auckland 1310, New Zealand
(a division of Pearson New Zealand Ltd)
Penguin Books (South Africa) (Pty) Ltd, 24 Sturdee Avenue, Rosebank, Johannesburg 2196, South Africa

Penguin Books Ltd, Registered Offices:
80 Strand, London WC2R 0RL, England

Cover image: *Girl with a Watering Can* by Pierre-Auguste Renoir, 1876. The National Gallery of Art, Washington, D.C. Photograph © Francis G. Mayer/Corbis; p.4 photo by Steven Lindblom.

Library of Congress Cataloging-in-Publication Data
Kelley, True.
  Pierre-Auguste Renoir : paintings that smile / written and illustrated by True Kelley.
    p. cm. — (Smart about art)
  ISBN 0-448-43371-0 (pbk.) — ISBN 0-448-43819-4 (hardcover)
  1. Renoir, Auguste, 1841–1919—Juvenile literature. 2. Painters—France—Biography—Juvenile literature.
I. Title. II. Series.
  ND553.R46K45 2005
  959.4—dc22
                                                                    2004011228

(pbk) 10 9 8 7 6 5 4 3 2 1
(hc)   10 9 8 7 6 5 4 3 2 1

Dear Class,

Our unit on famous artists is almost over. I hope that you enjoyed it as much as I did.

I am excited to read your reports. Here are some questions that you may want to think about:

🎨 Why did you pick your artist?

🎨 If you could ask your artist 3 questions, what would they be?

🎨 Did you learn anything that really surprised you?

Good luck and have fun!

Ms. Brandt

Renoir is pronounced "REN-WAHR"

Sometimes, before my piano lesson, I feel nervous (maybe because I haven't practiced much that week). I look at the cover of my music book, and I feel a little better. There's a picture of two girls at a piano. They look like they're having such a good time. The picture is by Auguste Renoir, and in lots of his paintings people are smiling and having fun. That's why I picked Renoir for my report. His paintings make me smile.

Practice makes perfect!

me at the piano with my friend

Young Girls at the Piano by Pierre-Auguste Renoir, 1892. Musée D'Orsay, Paris, France. Photograph © Herve Lewandowski, Réunion des Musées Nationaux/Art Resource, New York.

I wonder what song she's playing?

A KID CALLED AUGUSTE

Pierre-Auguste Renoir was born in 1841. (His parents always called him Auguste.) When Auguste was four, the whole family moved to an apartment in Paris. It was near the royal palace. Auguste and his friends played marbles or cops and robbers in the palace courtyard. Sometimes the queen of France would throw candy from her balcony to try to get them to quiet down. It sounds like they had fun.

Auguste

Everybody knew Auguste would be an artist someday. His dad was a tailor, and when Auguste was little, he'd take his dad's chalk and draw pictures of people and pets all over the walls and floors of the shop. His parents didn't really mind. But they figured they'd better get him some pencils and paper!

RENOIR THE DISH PAINTER

When he was thirteen, Auguste got a job painting china plates and vases. He learned to paint flowers first. He worked so fast, he made a ton of money for a kid. At lunchtime, he'd race over to the Louvre, a famous art museum in Paris, so he could study the great paintings there.

All done! Time for lunch!

But when somebody invented a machine to print pictures right on the plates, Auguste was out of a job.

ART SCHOOL DAYS

So Renoir went to art school. When he and his artist friends weren't painting, they liked to talk about painting. They thought that artists who wanted to paint landscapes should go outside and paint what they were looking at. That may not sound like such a big, new idea. But it was. Before this, artists stayed inside their studios to paint a picture of a lake or forest. One time when Renoir was out in the woods painting, he was so busy that he didn't notice a deer behind him, watching him work!

Self-Portrait by Pierre-Auguste Renoir, 1876. Fogg Art Museum, Cambridge, Massachusetts. Photograph © Bettmann/Corbis.

Self Portrait of Renoir

Look, it's not finished!

the French called painting outdoors "en plein air."

Olde Style Artists

1. They painted events in history or Greek and Roman legends.
2. They painted heroes, famous people, and gods and goddesses who all looked perfect and beautiful.
3. They liked dark colors and lots of detail.
4. They painted inside their studios.

New Style Artists

A TRAIN

WASHERWOMEN

1. They painted what they saw . . . even if it was a railroad bridge or an ugly factory.
2. They did portraits of ordinary people, happy or sad, doing everyday stuff like ironing or playing cards.
3. They used quick brushstrokes and bright colors and tried to paint what they saw at a glance.
4. They painted outdoors a lot.

SHOWTIME

Once, I traded a painting I did of the cobbler's wife for a pair of shoes.

The trouble was, nobody wanted to buy the new pictures that Renoir and his friends were painting. They were all broke. Any money they had, they spent on paint. They ate nothing but beans!

Back then, if artists in Paris wanted to make any money, they had to get their paintings into a special show called the Salon. The judges for the Salon were very strict and stuffy. They didn't care for the new style of painting. When Renoir finally got a picture into the show, it was hung way up high in the dark so people could barely see it. Even then, people made fun of it!

a fat woman daubed with white...

a nice semisoft cheese out for a stroll!

Don't be catty!

ha ha ha ha

ha h.

ha h

The devil of it is the light changes so quickly!

But Auguste kept right on painting the way he wanted. In 1869 he and his friend Claude Monet went to a popular restaurant called the Frog Pond. You could also go swimming there. They both made paintings of this same spot. Renoir's painting was done very fast and was kind of sketchy. But it seems to catch the lively feeling of the place, the people, the air, and the sunlight. Painting this way is hard. You have to paint fast because clouds move, shadows change, and in a minute the whole scene can look very different. The ripples in the water are just squiggly lines. But they still give the impression of moving water. Renoir and his friends became known as the Impressionists.

The Frog Pond (La Grenouillère) by Pierre-Auguste Renoir, 1869. Photograph © The National Museum of Fine Arts, Stockholm, Sweden.

See the guy untying the boat? The sleeping dog? The woman talking to the kid? Is she telling him not to cannonball someone?

MAKING A GOOD IMPRESSION

Without Monet, I would have given up!

In 1874 about thirty artists who couldn't get into the Salon held their own show . . . the first Impressionist show. Most people thought the show was a joke and that the artists were nuts!

This was one of Renoir's paintings in that show. Black was one of Renoir's favorite colors. That made him different from the other Impressionists. They didn't like to use black. A while after the show, Renoir tried holding an auction to sell Impressionist paintings. That didn't work either. Some art students attacked the paintings with sticks and umbrellas. The police came! I never thought pretty paintings could make people so mad!

The Theater Box (La loge) by Pierre-Auguste Renoir, 1874. Courtauld Institute Galleries, London, Great Britain. Photograph © Scala/Art Resource, New York.

The model was nicknamed "Fish Mouth".

Does her mouth look like mine?

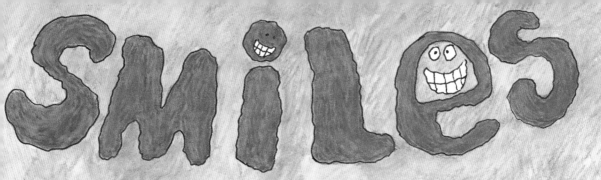

Did that stop Renoir? No! He went on making his beautiful, happy paintings anyway.

I love cats, so my aunt sent me this card with a Renoir painting on it. The girl was one of Renoir's favorite models. She died a few years after he did the painting. Renoir was very sad about that.

Woman with a Cat by Pierre-Auguste Renoir. 1875. The National Gallery of Art. Washington, D.C. Photograph © Francis G. Mayer/Corbis

Here's another card my aunt sent me.

Girl with a Watering Can by Pierre-Auguste Renoir. 1876. The National Gallery of Art. Washington, D.C. Photograph © Francis G. Mayer/Corbis

I think this card is very sweet, and I love the dress.

PARTY

This is my favorite Renoir painting. People are having fun at an outdoor dance. It is a big painting—six feet wide! Renoir's friends helped him carry the big canvas back and forth from his studio—not so easy on windy days!

Some of the people in the painting look like they're smiling right at me and asking if I want to come and dance, too. I wonder if Renoir stopped painting long enough to dance himself.

Ball at the Moulin de la Galette by Pierre-Auguste Renoir, 1876, Musée D'Orsay, Paris, France. Photograph © Réunion des Musées Nationaux/Art Resource, New York.

A lot of the people in the Painting are my friends.

The world knew how to laugh in those days!

Critics didn't like → these purple shadows that looked like clouds.

LUNCH TIME!

Look at all the different hats!

Cute dog! ↗

I think Renoir liked dogs.

This painting is called *The Luncheon of the Boating Party*. I love it because everyone looks happy and full after a good meal. The girl playing with the little dog is Renoir's girlfriend, Aline Charigot. She later became his wife, and he painted her a lot. When people met Aline, they thought she looked like a Renoir painting!

Is she covering her ears ← so she can't hear him? Or is she just fixing her hat?

RENOIR THE DAD

In 1885 Aline and Auguste had their first son, Pierre. Their second son, Jean, was born in 1894 and a third son, Claude (CoCo), was born in 1901. Now Renoir had his own family to use as models! They were a happy family. Renoir loved watching his children play.

Claude is playing with toy soldiers. That way, he sat still long enough to be painted.

Check out his long hair!

Claude Renoir Playing by Pierre-Auguste Renoir, 1905. Musée de l'Orangerie, Paris, France. Photograph © Réunion des Musées Nationaux/Art Resource, New York.

One funny thing about Renoir was that he worried a lot about his children. Of course, the kids weren't allowed to play with sharp things or matches. But Renoir also cut off the corners of tables and got rid of the sharp edges on all the furniture so they wouldn't hurt themselves. He was a worse worrier than my mom or dad.

Claude Renoir as a Clown by Pierre-Auguste Renoir, 1909. Musée de l'Orangerie, Paris, France. Photograph © C. Jean, Réunion des Musées Nationaux/Art Resource, New York.

I don't think Renoir's son liked posing in this silly clown costume!

Renoir also believed his kids should have lots of freedom. So they didn't go to school until they were ten! He figured they'd catch up!

Auguste Aline Pierre Jean Claude

The Renoirs bought a house in Aline's hometown in France. In 1894 Aline's cousin Gabrielle came to live with them and help take care of the children. She was Renoir's favorite model for many years.

Gabrielle and Jean by Pierre-Auguste Renoir, 1895. Musée d'Orsay, Paris, France. Photograph © Jean Schormans, Réunion des Musées Nationaux/Art Resource, New York.

Here are the nanny, Gabrielle, and baby Jean.

PEOPLE PAINTER

The Impressionist artists kept having shows. Most people just came to laugh at their paintings. But a few rich businessmen liked what they saw. They hired Renoir to do portraits of their families. Renoir was very likable, and he got more portraits to do by word of mouth.

That's Paul next to his mom! It was the fashion in those days to dress little boys like girls! No comment. Little Georgette is sitting on the Newfie.

Madame Georges Charpentier and Her Children, Georgette-Berthe and Paul-Emile-Charles by Pierre-Auguste Renoir, 1878. The Metropolitan Museum of Art, Catherine Lorillard Wolfe Collection, Wolfe Fund, 1907. (07.122) Photograph © 1992 The Metropolitan Museum of Art.

Here's a lady named Madame Charpentier with her children. They had to sit forty times for this painting! Madame Charpentier pulled some strings and got the painting into the Salon. It was a great success, and Renoir was on his way.

My purpose has always been to paint people as *if* they were beautiful fruit.

Renoir didn't do very many landscapes or still-life paintings (pictures of fruit or flowers).

Those black eyes look weird to me.

He didn't like to paint snow, either. He said, "Why paint snow? It's one of nature's illnesses."

Didn't he like snowball fights or sledding ???

Renoir liked painting people best. He liked to paint pretty pictures that would make people feel good when they looked at them. "There are enough ugly things in life for us not to add to them," he said. To me, a lot of Renoir's people, especially the women and girls, look alike. They have that same dreamy look. My mom thinks they look "icky-sweet," but I don't.

Mother and Children by Pierre-Auguste Renoir, 1875. © The Frick Collection, New York.

See the muff to keep her hands warm?

RENOIR THINKS HE CAN'T PAINT

Even great artists can think they're no good. Just when Renoir became successful, he started worrying that his paintings were bad. Maybe painting was getting too easy for him. So he started traveling. He went to Italy and visited museums with great paintings by Italian artists of the past. He was restless. He took long walks. Once he came to a river and couldn't get across it. Some peasant women picked him up, formed a line across the river, and passed him from one to another until he reached the other side!

Please pass Mr. Renoir!

By 1883 Renoir had changed the way he painted. His brush-strokes weren't so soft and feathery. The colors were duller. The people looked sort of stiff. He was trying to make his paintings look more like the ones he saw in Italy. I don't think it worked. Nobody bought the paintings. In art books, I read this is called Renoir's "Dry Period." But after a few years, Renoir decided to return to the old way of painting—soft and light—for good.

Half of this painting is done in the old soft style and the other half is the smoother darker style. Can you tell which is which?

This painting is called "Les Parapluies." That means "The Umbrellas."

← That's Aline with the basket. She has that dreamy look.

I was at a dead end.

RAIN-TING

By now, Renoir was famous all over the world. Then one day, when he was riding his bike, he hit a puddle, fell off, and broke his arm.

Luckily, he could paint as well with his left hand as with his right. Look! I sure can't do that! Can you?

right hand

left hand

Renoir got arthritis in his arms and hands, and it hurt! He took up juggling to try to exercise his sore hands. The arthritis got worse. He also had terrible toothaches and earaches. He had a stroke and was partly paralyzed. He had to be carried to his studio, and he painted from a wheelchair. Renoir said, "If I have to choose between walking and painting, I'd rather paint."

Pierre-Auguste Renoir Seated in Chair © Hulton-Deutsch Collection/Corbis.

OUCH! But I keep on painting!

age 71

Look at his poor hands...

When Renoir was 73, World War I broke out. Renoir's sons Jean and Pierre were wounded in the war. But worst of all, his dear wife Aline died suddenly at age 56. Renoir was sad, sick, and lonely.

JOIE DE VIVRE!

Still, he kept on painting. His hand was so crippled and claw-like that someone had to put the brush in it and take it out when he was done painting. But while he painted, Renoir was happy and hummed little tunes! You would never know he was in pain to look at the pictures! Amazing. I think Renoir painted the joy of living better than anyone. The French call it *"joie de vivre"* *(jwah duh veevr)*.

This is one of the last pictures I painted.

JOY OF LIFE!

Here's a painting Renoir did of the town in southern France where he lived for the rest of his life. It was sunny and warm there.

Terrace at Cagnes by Pierre-Auguste Renoir, 1905. Bridgestone Museum of Art, Tokyo, Japan. Photograph © Erich Lessing/Art Resource, New York.

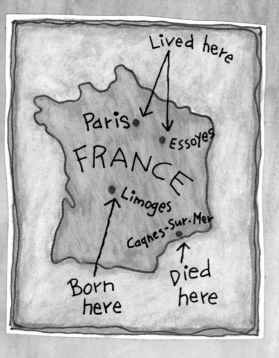

Lived here

Paris

FRANCE

Essoyes

Limoges

Cagnes-Sur-Mer

Born here

Died here

Renoir experimented with painting until the day he died, when he was 78. On that day he did a small picture of some flowers and said, "I think I'm beginning to understand something about this." He painted every day for sixty years. He painted about six thousand pictures!

Renoir lived to see one of his paintings hanging in the Louvre with all the great paintings he had looked at as a young man. Today, when I go to a museum and see his paintings, I notice other people looking at them. They are usually smiling, too.

THREE QUESTIONS I WISH I COULD ASK RENOIR:

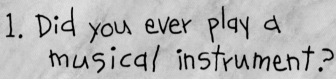

1. Did you ever play a musical instrument?

2. Did you have any pets?

3. Did you smile a lot?

Dear Winter,
   Your report made me smile.

(As you can see, I'm no artist!) Renoir's love of children shows through in his paintings, doesn't it?
   Ms. B.